For Kathy the love of my life:

five fifty
her soft in and out breath
breath of my love

A crow
has settled on a bare branch —
autumn evening

Basho (1644-1694)

Spring

a dark form
slow through the spring sky
great heron

when I doubt
a loving creator
the meadowlark

the old woman
shuffles through her tulips
spring in her eyes

silver drops of spring rain
wait to fall
from tips of pine needles

soft May morning
capped by a mare's tail sky
littered with flowers

my neighbor Mary
cradles her new granddaughter
the light in her face

morning
a breath of sweetness
lilacs

4

over Denver
two sheer white pelicans
ride the wind

silent . . . watching me
from across the alley
a pink dahlia

a pale moon hides
in gathering low clouds
then comes soft rain

song falls through
the morning silence
canyon wren

man and woman
he talks . . . she listens . . . cries
I feel their sadness

a crocus
blooms in leaf litter —
spring blessing

that elm slipped on
a sheer green camisole
last night

cirrus feathers
amble across spring day —
smell of lilacs

after spring rain
at each pine needle's tip
a green world

in her shoulders
the sorrows of the poor
cleaning woman

June luscious prairie
sprinkled with black and brown
calves lambs and fawns

the pup and I stop
to admire hollyhocks
distant temple bells

clouds gather
wind dances with trees
scent of rain

children's laughter
splashes in the window
sharing their joy

swallowtail
guzzles at red zinnias
too drunk to fly home

it's been so dry
a spider's spun her web
in the rain gauge

at koi pond
among wind-shaped pines
a flute's song

life blooms
amid last year's death
first crocus

spring morning
a dozen jonquils nodding
under scumbled sky

a flute-like song
calls the prairie to spring —
meadowlark

coffee with an old friend
watching
those ravens wind-surfing

angry gods growl
flick lightning all around —
and soft rains fall

yellow swatch
of grace brightens my day
swallowtail

smiles
spill from the hawthorn
chickadee

Summer

a cheerful voice
sings with the cicadas
evening cricket

radiant mother
cradles her newborn son
her miracle

the setting sun
paints clouds an orange mixed
from wildfire smoke

woman hits a deer
ambulance takes her away —
a sudden gunshot

sunset shower
becomes double rainbow
summer magic

in deep shade
of the hawthorn tree
pale green moss

last night the song
of the first cicada
summer's heat

black angus herd
wanders clean out of sight—
like the bison

a cicada's husk
six legs . . . veined transparent wings
silent summer song

head down
headed down the tree
what's up bird

watching me
from over the high wall
a tall sunflower

chickadees
fill the day with song
crickets the night

honey bee stings my leg
I help it
to become a Buddha

18

hummingbird
sun-glitter at corner
halo of wings

raging sunrise
ignites the horizon
gentles to pink

a miracle —
a dandelion fluff
floats by

high thin sky
gold wash on top branches
morning grace

small mother of pearl clouds
inlaid
on August morning blue

a small brown mouse
scoots along garden wall
the dog's asleep

like tectonic plates
day and night jolt each other
thunder rolls at dusk

summer evening
a dragonfly squadron
hunts mosquitos

three does five fawns
grace a prairie ridgeline
summer gift

dandelion seed
drifts past brilliant in sunlight
that thought I lost

cumulus east
splashed magenta and gold
prairie sunrise

the midnight silence
sneaks through the bedroom window
with a cricket's chirp

tinted by smoke
a pink mackerel sky
Montana burns

hungry mouse
eats under feeder —
thistle seeds

my morning chore list
fill feeders check the garden
drink in day's beauty

bright sunny face
beams from crack in concrete
new sunflower

thunderstorms
grumble as they pass
sound no fury

sun just down
July's heat slowly fading
first cicada sings

Fall

a quiet sunrise
tiptoes into city's sleep
single crow wakes . . . calls

against storm clouds
bright flash of white wings
passing egret

a fast jet chalks
a straight white line across
morning's blackboard

in a bowl . . . dead
mixed with glasses and keys
a honey bee

bits of night
sleep in the branches
of the pines

the rising sun
brushes gold on the trees
blesses the day

each day my shadow
grows
as sun hurries south

a mourning dove
coos in the far distance —
song of longing

side by side
Venus and the young moon
bring delight

autumn rain
falls sungold leaf by leaf
soon the world's awash

this morning
summer lies scattered
in the street

morning dark
tapping on window
rain

trees start
undressing
fall

bits of night
flee from the light
silent crows

a lone crow calls
sunset fills with silent crows
evening vespers

mare's tail fall days
the sound of sunshine crunching
under my boots

we step
into a cricket's song
silence

shards of sunlight
litter the patio
summer's end

around faint earthshine
the Moon's arms reach for Venus
celestial embrace

thin fingernail moon
low in the evening fall sky
arms filled with earthshine

two women
hands talking to eyes
dog listens

childhood cousin
last of my father's clan dies
the bell tolls for me

a stranger's face . . . but . . .
her eyes . . . her funny laugh
my memories

                              a lone crow
                              high on a bare branch
                              calling . . . calling . . .

a cricket sings
to an almost-full moon
a harvest song

buttermilk spilled
on cornflower blue sky
weather change

one red maple leaf
perched lightly on the grass
simple beauty

trilling calls
from a soaring vortex
ah! sandhill cranes

morning breeze
aids goldengrove's unleaving
leafclatter

                              the setting sun
                              touches curves of waving grass
                              graceful dancers

the pup and I walk
in brief afternoon shower
my shirt barely wet

Winter

long curve of grass
its shadow etched on snow
a simple grace

early sunbright
cobalt and cold degrees
snowfallglitter

a piece of blue sky
glows where it fell by the road
drenched in snowmelt

in winter's den
the cold knifes to the bone
sharpened by age

cirrus ribbons
tie a cornflower blue bowl
to the prairie

                              bright needle pulls
                              white thread through blue denim
                              morning contrail

yesterday's ridge
wandered off in the night
foggy morning

40

lenticular clouds
litter the afternoon sky
crows surf chinook winds

tonight's full moon
calls the sun to come north
winter solstice

panic of geese
explodes from the South Platte
eagle flaps past

41

snow falls
all day . . . and night
soft morning

                              alone
                              in snow gray sky
                              that crow

the new moon
embraces the old
with her smile

tall grass stems
winter dead but still hold
their graceful curve

pale peach alpenglow
softens mountain's sharp ridge line
takes my breath away

sunflower seeds
in the backyard feeder
sprout as finches

a crow lands
on black leafless branch
sun on its wings

                    a lone crow
                    calls . . . calls . . . calls . . .
                    then silence

sunlight flares
in the snow muffled day
a silent crow

gloomy day walk —
my dog brings along
the sunshine

wag of his tail
and a walk with my dog
cures my foul mood

flight for life
zooms low over the house
trailing prayers

tiny feathers
drift away on sunbeams
hoar frost

goose calligraphy
brushed across November skies
winter warning notes

bits of night
crisscross the end of day
scattered crows

About the Author

Art Elser's poetry has been published in *Blood, Water, Wind, and Stone, Owen Wister Review, High Plains Register, The Human Touch, Science Poetry, The Avocet, Vietnam War Poetry,* and *Proud to Be.* His chapbook, *We Leave the Safety of the Sea,* received the Colorado Authors' League Poetry award for 2014. A collection of his poetry in *High Plains Register* received the Colorado Authors' League Poetry award in 2016. His latest book of poetry is *A Death at Tollgate Creek* (2017).